When Our World Was Whole

When Our World Was Whole

Poems by

Elizabeth Weir

Cover design by Shay Culligan
Original cover art by Mandy MacLean, Glasgow, Scotland.
Sandhill Cranes at Dawn (watercolor).
mandy.maclean27@gmail.com.

ISBN: 978-1-63980-231-9

Kelsay Books
502 South 1040 East, A-119
American Fork, Utah 84003
Kelsaybooks.com

In gratitude to Chet Corey, friend, mentor, poet

Acknowledgments

Elizabeth Weir wishes to thank the publications in which the following poems appeared, some under other titles:

Adanna: "On the Greek Isle of Hydra," "Seen and Unseen"
Art Word Quarterly: "Autumn Encounter"
BoomerLit: "You Know Your Brother in Your Bones," "Coming Home on a January Evening"
Coe Review: "Bronzed Shoes on a Budapest Quayside"
Comstock Review: "Early in Nonsuch Park," "White-bottomed Wasp," "Awakening," "Reading the Daybook"
Crossings At Carnegie: "She Stood at the Door," "All That We Miss"
Evening Street Review: "Craft," "New Orleans Bronze," "Migrant," "Emigrating from England," "Intermission at Lee Blessing's Play, *Going to St. Ives,*" "Coal Delivery," "Francesca da Rimini," "Nightfall"
Gyroscope: "Conjuring Mary Oliver in Wolsfeld Woods"
The Kerf: "As Morning Fingers Off the Glove of Night," "Incubation," "From My Bedroom Window I See," "The Soul Is Rife with Contradiction," "Bird and Conscience Converge," "Called Down from the Sky"
Martin Lake Journal: "A More Intimate Gift"
Meridian Review: "The Day the Pandemic Was Declared"
Milkweed Editions, Voices for the Land: "Trespass"
Right Hand Pointing: "Major Service"
Talking Stick: "Springtime in Washington DC," "When Our World Was Whole," "Improbable"
Turtle Island Quarterly: "Listening with My Midwife Ear"

With Gratitude

This collection of poetry began to take form on Mallard Island at an artist retreat, thanks to the Oberholtzer Foundation, and found its voice a year later at Carolyn Light Bell and Lucy Bruntjen's Cranberry Lake retreat.

So many have helped to guide this second book forward, among them poets and friends, Sharon Chmielarz, Tracy Youngblom, June Blumenson, Carolyn Light Bell, Lucy Bruntjen, Susie Mackay and, most importantly, my sharp-eyed husband, Ken, who reads and advises on each newly penned poem.

Special thanks to poetry group friends, Tracy Youngblom, Janet Jerve, Marie Rickmyer, Kathy Weihe, Ann Iverson, Sandy Kacher, Kathleen Wedl, Beth Spencer, Diane Pecoraro and Cindy Wold; all have been instrumental in bringing *When Our World Was Whole* into being.

Contents

*You can find poetry
in your daily life,
your memory, on the bus,
in the news, or just
what's in your heart.*

—Carol Ann Duffy, poet

Early in Nonsuch Park

We watch her leave, and my dad
looks around—no park keepers.
"Now," he says. "Be quick."
He lifts me into the scented whiteness
of a May tree in full flower,
until I can see over the lip
of a mud-woven nest.
I'm lowered, and we back
through twigs and bee-hum
into the open and away.

"Four blue eggs," I whisper,
and a bare, squirmy thing."
"Well done; a hatchling."
We wait on a log to be certain
the thrush returns and see her flit
into the whiteness, worm in beak.
"Good, she's back. Come along,"
and he takes my hand—me,
stretching to match his stride,
he, with spring in his step.

Awakening

I'd sometimes spring from my bed
to watch their teamwork,
their sounds as dependable
as my mother's voice,
and wait for the clop of Bessie's hooves
as she hauled her laden milk cart
up the rise of Nonsuch Walk.
The great shire knew her route
as well as our milkman,
who could carry six full pints
in his hands, like fat white fingers.

I'd hear him crunch across the gravel,
set the bottles on our doorstep,
collect the clinking empties and call,
"Move along there, Bessie."
The horse blew into her nose bag,
strained harness creaking
as she leaned to drag the load
of rattling milk crates
to the Shaw's house next door.

I'd listen for wood pigeons to coo
their five-note sighs of affection
and, beneath my eiderdown,
I'd curl in the comfort of certainty,
unaware that within a year
Bessie would be gone,
replaced by an electric milk cart
that hummed and could not,
upon command, move along.

Mum's Forty-Third Birthday

We could hardly wait for her day
and had crossed the busy main road
(strictly forbidden) to gather armfuls
of poppies that grew in a remnant
wheat field on the edge of Nonsuch Park.
Home again, we nabbed her wash bucket,
filled it from Dad's rain barrel, stuffed in
the poppies and hid them in the bicycle shed.

She sensed that something was afoot,
we three tight with our big secret.
"I won't have anymore injured animals
to care for," she warned, "nothing alive."

Packed with excitement, we awakened
her next morning; she, uneasy.
Nicky led her, hand in hand, to the shed.
Trevor swung wide the door. "No, no!"
I cried—her metal bucket stood
in a crimson rosette of fallen petals.

"What a clever gift for my birthday,"
she said and knelt to show us the seed cups
with their black velvet caps, the pinholes
around each rim for the ripened seeds
to be tossed free by the winds of July.
"We'll let the seeds ripen, then shake
them over my flower bed and,
for my birthday this time next year,
I'll have a blaze of blooming poppies."

Coal Delivery

London, England, after WW II

Mother feared that the coal man
might deliver us one sack short
and told me to stand in the unheated
front room to count all ten sacks.

The slight man climbed aboard
his flatbed lorry, stacked
a double row of five bulging burlap
bags along its near edge, jumped down
and heaved the first onto his back.
He staggered, found his balance
and lugged it through our side gate.
I heard the rumble of tipped coal
as he poured it into our empty bin.
Soon bored, I lost count and practiced
handstands against a bare wall.

He tapped at our kitchen door
to be paid. I'd neglected my job
but ran to join my mum.
She counted out careful pounds,
shillings and pence to give him.
I saw how stooped he was, yet young,
not so much older than me,
his clothes, cloth hat, the skin
of his face and hands engrained
in coal dust, his back bent beneath
the weight of limited possibility.

A Distant Day in April

Influenza Pandemic, 1957

On string legs, weak from influenza,
Mother supporting my elbow,
I stepped through our French windows
into an English spring garden.

Wrapped in a torrent of thrush song,
the day floated in stilled perfection,
dew-silvered lawn spongy underfoot.
I trod gingerly to avoid coiled worm casts.

Mummy led me to three deck chairs
set beneath our orange-pippin apple tree,
where my father puffed his Players Navy Cut,
its smoke curling through clusters of blossom.

In the gentle hum of foraging bees, he rose,
ash flittering, and tucked a blanket
around my knees. Mum brought two cups of coffee
and nourishing honey-barley water for me.

Pale sun dappled through the fragrant canopy,
warming my upturned face, and I drifted,
drowsy in the comfort of affection, listening
to quiet talk of parsnips and petunias

and knew I would hold this moment forever.
Now, on a cold April morning in middle-age
in another land, I sip this sustaining draught
as I convalesce from my first Minnesota winter.

Thirteen and Uncertain

Vegetables, my dad swore, would see us
through the thin years, post-war. His sure hand
nurtured seedlings summers-long, onions,
parsnips and potatoes, carrots and cabbages.
After the frosts of autumn, he'd come home
from his office job in London, tug on boots
and through the muddy chill of English winters,
breath steaming, dig foot-length rows for dinner.

I was thirteen and falling out of love with my dad.
He was unlike other fathers, with his teakwood
cigarette holder and fresh rose buttonhole.
I worried what my friends would think
of his large ears and habit of humming, but still
I loved the sweetness in his mashed parsnips.

The Clemency of Home

Mother and I sit on the garden step
as I tell of my new life as a student nurse,
of bottom-warm bedpans, soiled sheets,
lifting and turning heavy patients,
learning to hold kidney dishes to catch
vomit and not to retch, myself—
needs too many in a ward of pain.
I want to give up. Mum taps my hand,
insists I continue for at least a year. I tell
of Staff Nurse Bartle's scorn, scalpel-sharp.

Dad's roses bloom, their scent sweet
after weary hospital air. "Look,"
Mum laughs, "here comes autumn,"
as up the garden, fur frowsy with dust
and dead leaves, strolls Danny, our cat,
elderly now. He climbs onto her lap,
turns, purrs and kneads her skirt.
"Oh, Dan," she says, picking leaves
from his coat, "I washed and ironed
this yesterday," and the clemency
of home wraps me in its quilt.

The Fabric of Family

I wouldn't have called it burlap—
not exactly. No. It was more
common cotton, thin thread,
a bit worn, but comfortable.

By chance, silk happened along.
Charming, yes, a cocoon of love
and new well-being but, oh,
the effort to keep it pressed.

If you are cotton, true to your core,
can you ever do more than
slip on filmy silk, assume
your place with learned grace?

Bond

Other people's babies do not enchant me.
I fear I might not love my child but do love
our Delft-eyed, earless cat, a good sign, surely.

A persimmon sun hangs in the west.
I laze hot and ripe beneath our guava tree,
knowing tomorrow I'm to become a mother

You enter the world like Caesar. Woozy
from anesthetic, I fight nausea and pain
to look at you, creamy bundle. You fit

the crook of my arm. I stroke your cheek,
you nose toward my finger-touch
and something feral wells—

let nurse come to carry you away
and I'll hiss and spit, claw and yowl
to keep my young beside me.

I Cherish All of You

After Ann Ginsburgh Hofkin

From love we made you,
an original, our first creation.

I gaze at you lying in my lap,
those serious eyes, not mine,
perhaps your grandfather's,
mouth, your daddy's,
delicate ears, Auntie Ida's.
The tilt of your nose, my gift
and, in your imperious gaze,
Grandmother Violet.

You stretch a hand,
square and practical
as my mother's, and I know
we have plagiarized.

Emigrating from England

I pack long underwear for extreme cold,
boots and woolly jumpers, skirts, sandals,
and Indian cotton for summer heat,
Lego for the boys and favorite books,
A. A. Milne for them, Jane Austen for me,
wrap binoculars in soft cottons, fit in a guide
to the common birds of North America,
photos of my mother, brothers and sisters-in-law.
I tuck in the sound of cricket, willow bat
striking red leather ball on Oxted village green,
the joyful yelps of young cousins chasing
around my brother's rose beds,
the song thrush, on the roof peak,
closing day and this life I know. I pack
my mother's voice, our stomach-sadness.
Bundle it tight. Stuff it in. Shut the lid.
Mark the case: "FRAGILE."

"Please Mind the Gap"

Warning on the London Underground

Always that gap
between platform and train,
that potential trip
as you step
from where you are
to where your life
is taking you.

And when you arrive,
bereft of the comfort
of context, the gap gapes,
an absence, a trap
over which you
must aim
to—leap.

On Being New in Minnesota

I don't like how a hooked fish flips and wags,
tries to swim foreign air, a creature tugged
from its element, as I've been from mine.
My husband pursues his career in long hospital hours,
while our boys and I romp in snow's frozen hold,
until fierce cold forces us indoors to Lego, books,
the newness of television and Sesame Street.

Neighbors leave and return to sealed homes in cars,
our road, lonely. America's drive for profit
intrudes with multiple 'phone calls, urging me
to purchase triple pane windows, a family burial plot,
a timeshare in Florida, manly voices addressing me
as Beth and Betty, as though we're old chums.

Fergus begins preschool, his accent too soon
unlike mine. America claims him, vowel by vowel,
and I want to reel him in, keep him an apple-cheeked
English boy, to better hold on to who I am.
Torn from context, colors dulling, I sense
I'm swimming upstream in the wrong river.

Doorway

"Work is the key," advises my friend from South Africa.
She's recent, like me, and unsettled.

I rise to study before the boys awaken, pass the RN exam,
find a babysitter and fill part-time evening shifts.

Her suggestion sets me on a path toward a closed door
as I struggle to enter the immensity that is America.

I apply to a local newspaper and report
on school board and county commission meetings,

am given an arts beat, covering theater, dance, galleries,
book signings, and a key slips into the lock; it turns.

Dancing Ground

"Lek," a bird's courting ground

Me, in this canvas blind before dawn.
You, at home, warm beneath down.
Cold. Very cold. Sleet in driving wind.
Dawn leaks charcoal through heavy cloud.

A motor-whir of wings. Two-note cooing,
clucks and chuckles. Eleven sharp-tailed grouse,
bent upon amour, dip necks, arch stiff wings,
erect white-ruffed tails, shuffle fast feet,

each defending his invisible dancing ground.
All rattle quills, billow purple neck sacs, puff
orange brows—oh, what lady sharp-tailed grouse
can resist such ardent displays of love?

I rub purple-cold hands, shiver chilled flesh,
long to drop into the warm lek of your bed.

You Know Your Brother in Your Bones

One o'clock. Dirt on the windowpane.
I fetch *Windex* and a soft cloth.
Autumn colors blaze beyond—
a slight stirring of ochre and umber
as when a thought ruffles through.
Time gutters. Glass,
the bank of trees, recedes.
Thoughts of you,
my youngest brother,
far away in England,
crippled by slipped discs,
lying in a dulled haze of pain, daylong,
surviving interminable nights,
your life, wasting.
Memories of stacking logs together,
birdwatching in the reed beds
of Mote Park, beech trees ablaze
with autumn. Time, slipping between us—

Brief Sighting

After Tracy Youngblom

From beyond the hill comes the call, "Cuckoo, cuckoo."
The sound floats on English air. A flash of wings

and here it is, perched above me on a telephone pole.
Spring wraps a windy arm around my shoulders, and—

I'm a child again, walking in Nonsuch Park
with my father. "It's a strange thing," he'd tell me,

"you'll never see a Cuckoo. You'll only ever hear it."
Yet here it is, in plainest view, white spots

on its under-tail, my father, with me.
The shy bird churrs, "Kruk-kruck," and scimitars into wind.

Citizenship Ceremony

I volunteer on a political campaign to elect
a county commissioner, help her gain office
and begin to think about being able to vote.
That thought lingers for seventeen more years.

Among eager citizens, brand new, their faces
lit with joy, I hesitate on the threshold
feeling lonely for family and country.
I'm not yet ready to celebrate but, belonging
now, in two countries, I step over the sill.

At Wayzata Library

I pull the long, velvety sock onto my arm.
It has stalk eyes, a Sesame-Street gape
and a coil of soft fabric.
"Hello, little Satya," it says.
Our grandson's eyes grow soft.
"Am I a rabbit?" it asks, eager to know.
"Nope," and Satya shakes his head.
"Then I must be a mouse."
"No, no, no!" he squirms.
I hitch up the flop of fabric at my elbow.
"Perhaps I am a goat?"
"Nope." His eyes shine. The library,
bookshelves, other toddlers cease
to exist in his engaged present.
"I don't know who I am,"
my arm laments; the sock
twists its mouth into glumness,
droops its head, eyes
sagging, and sobs to itself.
Concern clouds Satya's person.
He points to the coil at my elbow.
"You am a snail," he tells the sock,
patting my arm.
The puppet lifts it head.
"A snail! I'm a snail!"
It nuzzles his neck, asks,
"Are you a snail, too?"
Satya shakes his head. "I am a boy."
"I like you," the sock tells him,
and he hugs my arm, hard.
He's as free from time and being
as breeze-blown thistle seed.

A City Official Opens Her Poetry Jotter

and finds a formula: The budget
is what the city needs to spend.
The levy is the money needed
to support the budget,
minus other fees and income.

Property tax is the assessed value,
multiplied by the class rate,
divided by the total tax capacity.
Combine the levy and the property tax
and you have the total tax rate.

Add a contentious election, chambers
packed with restless residents,
multiply by regular packets, fat with data,
divide by keeping house and husband,
and you have a poet soul
slipping into intractable deficit.

Anniversary

As the old year faded,
I sobbed
for my lost mother
into fur soft and warm
and firm. Boda bore
my raw emotion,
tail thumping,
fond eyes alight.

A year and one day later,
I sob into Boda's fur
soft and warm and slack,
her tail limp,
eyes dulling.
I have put down
the one who loved me
as a mother.

Major Service

You are at Mayo's famous
Body and Spare Parts Shop,
here for an aortic valve
and seal job, your old valve
worn and leaking, your pump
enlarged from working too hard.
From their tool bench, your team
selects a Sapien Three valve,
guides it along a major duct,
seats it with fine precision
and inflates it in place.
The team tests for patency
pressure, function. Job complete.
They park you in progressive care
where I come, spilling gratitude,
to collect and drive you home,
retooled and roadworthy.

Coming Home on a January Evening

Stamping off snow and darkness,
we enter the warmth of home,
wood-burning stove radiating heat.
The standing lamp and wing chair
invite me to settle and take up my book
left open on the pine-wood chest.
Root-knotted within its pot,
our forty-four-year-old fig tree
canopies over the worn couch,
still sporting shoots, green and tender.

Together, we've made this space,
a charmed place of clement weather,
deepness between us, unspoken.
I fear things that have yet to happen:
one of us confused by what a light switch is for,
the hidden billow of a ruptured blood vessel,
our fig tree failing, stove cold, lamp unlit—
Love when I hear no answer . . .

She Stood at the Door

Babs Chesler, April 4, 2015

We hug farewell, wheeled walker
awkward between us,
her bones, too present
within my arms,
dark eyes
deep with leavings.

I step away, into an early
San Antonio morning
through a chill mist
to a waiting taxi,
trailing a suitcase
packed with separations—
our left-behind countries,
mothers, loved animals
and, now, this last parting.

Through the taxi window,
I crane for connection.
She waves, her familiar face
no longer clear, shape
already diffuse in gray light.

Nightfall

For my brother, Trevor, Covid-19

Late winter sun slants low
over our lake, clothing the far shore
in chestnut light. A doe treks
through snow to nibble at dead
hydrangea heads, and a buck,
one antler already shed, follows.

Great-horned owls spill
hollow notes into diminishing light,
their muted calls soft as feathers
in silent flight. Darkness enfolds
owls and deer, garden and house
in ready arms as his heart falters.

To the vase of weary tulips
in his room of sighs, to his breath
that labors, let nighttime fall.
A chorus of coyotes keens,
then fades into stillness,
and a waning moon sets.

Improbable

Improbable that I should pass by
at the moment
a dragonfly alights on
the wing of a dragonfly sculpture,
a lone piece of art, planted
in a Minnesota prairie.

Improbable that I should be here,
in distant Minnesota, with you,
that you should have come, uninvited,
to a Polish party in South Africa,
that we should have met,
you from Ireland, me from England.

Improbable that I should happen to land
on the apex of your cardiologist heart
that long-ago night, that we are here,
contented, far from our origins
among summer prairies, sun-glanced
wings, unlikely sculptures.

Cross When You Can

My father taught me how to jaywalk busy London streets.
I'd meet him for lunch, on my days off from nursing,
and we'd stroll down The Haymarket, through Waterloo Place,
with its heroes of Empire proud on their plinths—
Britain still great in 1963—and cross The Mall
into St. James' Park, away from the London rush.
In this quiet spot, with its view over the lake,
we'd share his preferred bench. He'd unwrap
his lunch, a surprise each work day, sandwiches
made by my mother, crusts removed,
ham and mustard his hope, cheese and chutney mine,
enough for me, the begging ducks and pigeons
and, if we were lucky, a piece of her shortbread.

Now, as a visitor in 2019, I am relearning his skill:
look left in England. Not right. Take care though—
it's not always so. I'm retracing familiar footsteps but find
every park bench packed, paths swarming with people,
his lake view obscured by overgrown shrubbery.
I press my way to the footbridge spanning the lake,
where he liked to share his favorite London vista
along the length of lake to the fairy-castle view
of spired Whitehall, seat of government, that seems
to rise out of the leafy grounds of the park, an illusion.
I'm jaywalking life's surging traffic, yearning
to cross long decades to a treasured affection,
eyes brimming in the wake of my father's gaze.

*Patriarchy is like
the elephant in the room.
How can it not
affect life when it's
the superstructure
of human society?*

—Ani DiFranco,
songwriter and singer

New Orleans Bronze

Jean Baptist le Moyne de Bienville stands tall,
chin tilted, frock coat lifted in a Louisiana breeze,
breeches tied above determined calves.
He holds a staff and scroll, lands gained
with a fresh thumbprint.

Behind the honored founder, a priest
in sack-cloth robe, heavy rosary
hanging from his waist, face impassive,
his work done.

Seated below them both, a Chickasaw chief,
features finely cut, deep-set eyes down-cast,
his people's peace pipe empty in his hand.

Bronzed Shoes on a Budapest Quayside

*In Memory of Victims Shot into the Danube by Nazi Militiamen
1944–45*

Jewish shoes, weary, worn and worked, broken walled,
broken-willed shoes. Buttoned, buckled, ribboned
and strapped shoes. Sensible flats, fashion shoes,
pointed and patterned, a man's battered work boots.

Knee boots, torn and fallen, children's shoes,
paired and single. One heeled dancing-shoe tipped over,
a woman's sandals, small-boy shoes beside hers;
a man's lace-up leather shoe, its sole already over the edge.

Springtime in Washington DC

Pillars soar to the portico of the Supreme Court Building
where blind justice stands, weighing her impartial scales.

In the set perfection of the High Court's gardens,
a mockingbird casts his song over starry dogwoods,

and white pansies, brilliant in dulled light, nod to the pock
of constant rain. Blossom-smothered azaleas froth

around a bench of carved marble, heavy
with a man huddled beneath a sodden blanket.

Nine Minutes and Forty-Eight Seconds

George Floyd, 5/25/20

This is what it takes
to hold a Black man down,
face crushed to pavement,
for a white officer to knee
his weight onto a black neck,
hands in pockets, casual, kneeling,
kneeling, until the job is done.

This is what it took
for the world to know
the fear of living Black and male
in USA: a girl happening past
Cup Foods, her chanced video,
posted on social media,
of murder on a summer street.

This is what it took:
Darnella Frazier's courage,
her innocence in court
to counter reports
of officer lives threatened,
a "medical incident,"
to jerk our world awake.

Francesca da Rimini

A Pre-Raphaelite painting by William Dyce

How it still goes on, this age-old tendering
of young women for convenience, profit and pleasure.

Francesca's father strikes a bargain on the head
of his young daughter to settle a dispute, betrothing

her to an elderly, crippled nobleman. Obedient
to her father's will, Francesca marries Giancotto

and meets comely Paolo, her husband's young brother.
Francesca has read to Paolo, her book open in her lap.

Paolo has sung to her, his ribboned lute propped
against the parapet, his sweet tenor as intoxicating to her

as secretly sipped wine. Demure, yet lit with love
Francesca awaits the press of Paolo's urgent lips.

Behind, Paolo, unseen by both, her husband's jealous hand
grips the parapet, their futures, masked in darkness.

Little wonder Dyce painted a twilit background
of a nubile crescent moon, dogged by weighty Jupiter.

Craft

Bonsai means
a tree in a shallow dish
a tree like any other with the potential
for space, sky, light and life . . . This tree
has been root-pruned, like a foot-bound
girl-child, limbs trained for elegance
of form, undesirable growth
plucked away, until it is an
exquisite miniature of itself
a fine possession
convenient and
small, a
thing
to be
prized
and kept indoors.

It's That Look

There's a look a man gives
when it lingers and burns
strips with carnal eyes
intention implied and
a woman senses
she's the object
of his entitled
lust—knows
she must
leave . . .
if she
can.

Force

Trumpeter swan banding in Baker Park

I pinion her in strong arms,
clawed webs bloody my thighs,
wings thrash air,
two fight-shredded sails.

"A swan surrenders
if you grip her tight," the men
instruct, "once she knows
you mean to have your way."

In the vise of my arms,
her heart hammers beneath
down and fine bone,
her black beak brushes my ear.

She hisses a sigh. Fight dulls
in the jet of her feather-fringed eye.
She trembles in my arms, and I know
the swell of sudden possession.

Intermission at Lee Blessing's Play,
Going to St. Ives

"Would you help to kill a brutal dictator?"
a man beside us asks his companion
in the lobby of Park Square Theater.
We have been watching a woman doctor
wrestle with whether she should aid
in poisoning a ruthless African dictator.
His companion hesitates. *I'm not sure.*
"Surely you'd have helped to stop Hitler
if you'd known your decision would prevent
appalling cruelty and save millions of lives?"
She twists her scarf and avoids his gaze.
"You mean to say you don't know how you'd act?"
Once you've killed, she says, *it invites a next time,
to back up the purpose of the first. Look at Macbeth
and how one murder led to a string of killings.*
"That's historic fiction. Your ambivalence surprises me."
*For me to kill another would compromise the core
of who I am. I couldn't continue to live with myself.*
"Personal well-being becomes irrelevant, here.
We're talking about millions of human lives."
*In a dictatorship, others, hungry for power
and as corrupt as the dictator, will fight to fill the void.
How many others will I be required to kill?*
"I thought I knew you. You're not reasoning well."
She sets her chin and faces him. *Absolute certainty,*
she says, *underpins the thinking of every dictator.*
A bell sounds. It's over.

On the Greek Isle of Hydra

The heady smell of crushed oregano and thyme
beneath our feet scents the heating air
as we hike a rocky path, trodden by pilgrims
to a monastery high in the hills,
the sun already hot at this early hour.
The farther we climb, thirst plagues us.
Our guide assures, the monks will provide.

We pass through monastery gates,
and Evangelos raps on wooden doors.
A young monk in a brown habit answers,
beckons to our men and bars the women,
eyes downcast to avoid looking at us.
Heavy doors close. A latch clanks.

We wait in the parched shade of an olive tree
until our men return bearing beakers
and a pitcher of chilled well water.
We drink and drink, forgive the slight
to our gender, conscious of our power—
certain as the moon's pull that impels
ocean tides to rush the thighs of the land.

Apple Honored Eve

The Company took pilloried Eve's
apple, added a pert leaf at its stem,
and celebrated her bite into
the crisp flesh of knowing.

How grateful I am for her initiative
in that dreamed garden
of the male imagination
that created a myth to hold
womanhood culpable
for mankind's failings.

Within that tale, she gave us
the ability to analyze and deduce,
to grow in thought and to manage
the world for our species' advantage.
With her original gift, we groomed
grasses to fatten and provide grain,
invited cattle into care and treachery,
harnessed the horse, conceived
machines to speed the wheels
of commerce, soared
to the moon, invented technology
to tap the universe, and produced
this Apple iBook computer
upon which, today, I doodle.

Eclipse at Starbucks

She's slight, the girl in front of me,
the line, long, barista, slow.
He works, impassive as a machine.
I cannot see her face. From the back,
a loose rope of fair hair coils
over her collarbone, disappears
into the bosom of her sweatshirt.
The line shuffles forward.
Bored barista eyes engage.
She orders: grande cappuccino.
Lashes skim mahogany cheeks
as he leans towards her,
makes her repeat her order.
His shoulders broaden,
chest puffs, narrow hips taut.
He returns her change,
fingers lingering in contact.
Leaning across the counter,
he points to where her coffee will be,
perhaps, to catch the scent of her.

It's my turn: small latté, decaffeinated.
He takes my money, calls, "Next."
Coffee in hand, I look to see
the face that so awakened him.

She's gone. I glimpsed the moon's
unlit curve, missed its shining round.

Grace on Bourbon Street

She sets up in the middle of Bourbon Street,
among painted tourist carriages and unhurried cars,
slowed by a four-way stop.

Mule carriages clop to a halt, bassist tum, tum, tumming.
Drivers turn off engines, wind down windows,
drummer pulsing staccato,

guitarist's humming strings, her voice a rope of honey,
hugged along aged brick houses and given back—hot gospel,
rising among wrought iron balconies.

Tourists crowd, rapt by her round of want and longing
and, as one, we are steeped in her chalice of sound.
Police gather, shoulders swaying.

Foot, tap, tap, tapping, she lets the music ride,
picks up a battered clarinet, throws back her head and blows,
a madonna in full carol.

She sets aside her clarinet, drummer, barely brushing.
Buckets pass, purses spring, and congregants shift,
awkward—awakened—

proximity too close in a crowd of strangers. Police press in,
chivvy mules and tourists on and, like beads on a broken rosary,
we spill and scatter.

Migrant

Bruno Catalano sculpted bronze and air

Catalino's figure of a man trudges.
From one angle, he seems whole—
his two legs, head and shoulders,
left arm, carrying a small case, present.

Missing, his right side—central core—
his country—kin—his way of life—
                                    a gape of air—

All That We Miss

Namaqualand, Namibia, Southwest Africa

We hurry into the setting sun in search of Namaqualand's brief
promise of a desert strewn with the hues of sudden daisies.

Disappointment thrums beneath our tires; a few snatches
of color here and there as on we speed, blind with haste,

our habit to search and consume, never enough time
to know the world and live in its gift. I had pictured

carpets of color, bee-hum and wonder. We throttle on, hot
and irritated in lessening light, grumbling at this late gamble

to witness a desert in bloom, when I thumb through our guide,
read, "Namaqua daisies turn to face the sun," and glance

in the sideview mirror—behind us lies a coral-colored vastness,
stretching beyond the numbing miles we have spent. We stop,

stand, stunned by the beauty around us and watch as ephemeral
desert flowers fold their petals against the coming darkness.

And Earth
is but a star
that once
had
shone.

—James Elroy Flecker, poet

These Woods Hold Silences

Deep in winter woods a flick
of movement, a fox circling the base
of a great maple. It rushes the tree, runs
at the trunk and drops back. Again.
And again. Fox sits, alert, nose
pointed upwards, tries once more,
gives up and mooches off.

Perhaps there's a meal up the tree,
trapped between two perils.
My tea, too hot to sip. All is still, until
a gray squirrel scoots down the trunk,
dashes over open snow—swoop—
wide wings—a Red-tailed Hawk
locks the squirrel in dagger talons.

Minutes pass, furred tail twitching.
Morning tea grows cold. Hawk grips—
cold intimacy of death, the double helix
of prey and predator intertwined,
each designed for the possibility
of the other. Hawk lifts into flight,
a banner of gray tail streaming behind.

From My Bedroom Window I See

two rag piles dropped in morning snow. One pulls out
                        a nose; snuffs the air.

It stands, stretches front, then back legs,
                        ashy tail curling,

shakes off night and trots, confident onto the wastes
                        of the winter-stiff lake.

The second pile rouses, looks around. They belong.
                        This land has always been theirs.

Our tender grandbaby stirs in her crib as the coyote cocks
                        a proprietary leg against our maple.

He glances towards the house, balances on three legs
                        to scratch his feral jaw.

I picture summer and our grandbaby crawling among clover,
                        hungry eyes watching.

Dread erupts, red as fang-torn flesh. I fling up the sash
                        and yell into frozen air.

The baby startles and cries—coyote tips his head
                        ears flicking to catch her cry.

The Clean Page of the Day

Dawn opens to hush and new snowfall,
an invitation to idle snowshoes.

Cutting deep into whiteness,
I huff down the hill

to the unwritten lake, breath pulsing
great bursts of mist, free and first out—

but not first scribe this virgin morning.
I find the perfect imprint of a bird,

wings mantled wide, pinion feathers
bladed in detail, and a hole

where talons punched through
to a bright spot of crimson blood—

signature of the Great Horned Owl,
a tale, with an ending, penned in snow.

A Late Winter Walk in Wolsfeld Woods

Wolsfeld, but a remnant of what used to be,
my companions soaring oaks,
maples, bass and ironwoods,
the native cover for this land.
The song of the wind plays
their bare branches and,
below my path a stream,
swollen with snowmelt, gushes
in a deep ravine. An owl,
disturbed by my presence, wings
across the open space
to alight in a maple on the far side.
The bird hoots a four-note call,
"Who cooks for you?" Its mate
answers, "Who cooks for you, all?"
Together, they fuel a din of indignation
that resonates through the vaults
of their wooded home. Well scolded,
I hasten from their concern,
comforted by the grace of great trees.
Unseen, a woodpecker tap-taps
a resonant bough. Too soon,
I reach the woodland's edge
to re-enter the mangled lands of man,
loud and jangled, and sense
the thinness of the world.

Listening with My Midwife Ear

Overhead, a woodpecker drums resonant wood—
bare March branches, but no movement.

Again, the wood-bell rap, a distinct sequence,
repeated and amplified by a hollow tree limb,

this not a drilling for insects, not a nest excavation,
but a declaration of territory, an appeal to a female.

Spring slumbers beneath knee-deep snow
but the sun's arc rises, awakening desire.

I clomp to a Scots pine and press my ear to its rough trunk.
All I hear is the outer world of aircraft and passing cars.

At the next tree, an old linden, I find the curve of a burl, risen
like a pregnant belly. I set my midwife ear against its swell,

and hear his fervor, feel the promise in our turning Earth
as down the length of lignum the woodpecker's rap quickens.

The Day the Pandemic Was Declared

March 11, 2020

Beyond breakfast and my kitchen window,
a Red-tailed Hawk landed, awkward, on the lawn.
I watched it hesitate, spring upwards, legs extended
to clutch at something unsuspecting in the grass.
The hawk rose, a garter snake writhing
in its talons, flew to a bare branch and tore
at the head. The flailing lash of tail stilled
as the hawk ripped chunks of flesh, gulping
them down. The snake had been basking
in warm sun when death darted in.

In a Time of Contagion

Long displaced by human growth,
kangaroos explore Sydney suburbs,
jackals saunter Teheran's broad avenues,
and dolphins frolic in Venetian canals.
Residents of Beijing, Shanghai
and Delhi marvel at blue skies,
unseen for a generation

In polished nights, Venus gleams bright
and airplane-free skies open to the sounds
of swans and geese winging north,
Red-wings and Robins belling peaceful air,
the roar of rushing roadways, hushed.
In a time of hallowed quiet,
our damaged planet breathes.

As Morning Fingers Off the Glove of Night

three plump shapes perch
on a log, silhouetted
against a wind-scuffed lake.

The sun slips free of the horizon
and they're Canada geese
shrugged-up against morning cold.

The middle bird has drooping wings,
one wing more dropped than the other.
Injured, I assume. Won't do well.

Hours later, I check again.
Two birds have left the log
to forage close by.

The middle bird stands, stretches
wings and reveals three pairs
of spiky legs—week-old goslings.

Night-long she's sheltered them
in the warm muff of her wings, kinship
instant, her need to nurture, familiar.

The Soul Is Rife with Contradiction

Morning time
I ease countless caterpillars
off my ravaged roses,
innards petal-pink
through pearly skin.
They hollow out
whole rosebuds, strip
prickly twigs naked.
Stumpy legs cling
to my fingers,
heads still searching
to stuff themselves
with airy ambition.
I toss plump bodies
into hungry woods.

Evening time
In opalescent light,
a sunset flock
of black swallowtails
drink from seeping rock,
wings opening and closing.
Settled butterflies
are radiant petals,
velour-soft wings,
limned in crimson,
hindwings, garlands
of crescent moons.
They flower around me—
I'm haloed in happiness.

A More Intimate Gift

At White Water Draw, Arizona

We rise in the Tucson dark
and arrive at flooded desert flats
to be there with a guide
when the sun uncorks his jar of light.
We expect to witness acres
of seared winter reeds lift
into a croaking rush of Sandhill Cranes.
In awakening light, we wait.

Wetlands hunker, still and silent.

Our guide's promised phenomenon
has failed. He apologizes as ten Willets,
sharp as shot arrows, zip past our noses,
wheel and settle in shallows at our feet.
On stilt legs, they murmur to each other
as they sift the pond for mud-loving larvae,
unbothered by us or our expectations,
these long-billed shorebirds, winter-gray.

Evening Under a June Quarter Moon

My granddaughter and I stroll
in veiled moonlight, stars concealed
beyond Long Beach's tired air,
one planet, faint through the haze
as we cross the low lagoon bridge.

In the receding tide, teeming
dashes of neon, each scrolling
within a trail of phosphorescence.
We drop to our knees, dip
wary hands into black sea water
shot with swirls of light.

                Imagine—
this splendor in our lives,
we might have passed them by,
these fiery creatures of the tide—
so much we miss, so little we know.

White-bottomed Wasp

Summer-long we meet at the clothesline.
Up go my husband's shirts.
Down go her jaws as she cuts
fibers from a wooden clothespin.

I hang my blue denim skirt and marvel
at her narrow waist, thin as wire,
note the blonde tip to her segmented tail,
the yellow-lined shield of her thorax.

Jaws packed tight, she leaves
to chew wood into pulp,
and I note shallow grooves
scooped into my weathered pins.

Soon she returns, or another just like her.
How I admire her industry—
envy her inborn skill to build
something complex from simple matter.

At day's end, when I collect the washing,
she's still there, harvesting wood
among pins softened by rain and sun,
new pins, untouched.

In Autumn, the work of this small artisan
dips into view on a leafy twig-end of sugar maple—
a parchment globe of spittle and daub
purled into walls of gray and cream.

Its fluted canopies, fashioned
perhaps for show, perhaps for shade,
glow translucent in low sun, and I long
to craft something, anything so fine.

Reading the Day Book

I stop to read the messages on the night stone.
Blank this morning. I splash it myself.
My man's whistling. Already. He wants me beside him,
but I have work to do, a whole night to decipher.
I smell an old fox; he crossed into the woods.
I follow his line to the oak tree he marked
and make it my own. Another strong lead:
deer pellets—hmm. I lick down a few and roll in the rest.
He's at it. Again. All right. I'll be there—in a minute.
Geese on the field. I freeze, ready to chase
but new information distracts my attention:
warm bird; strong and close, in the long grass.
It's mine, if—I'm—careful. In I dash—it explodes
in my face, a pheasant, a flyer, the rotten cheat.
Better catch up. Don't want to be leashed.
Yes, yes. I cock my leg. Still he insists.
I bounce up to him, smile and wag my tail.
I've got to buy time, the page is so rich.
We're off, again, my nose to the ground.
The retriever next door squatted right here.
I water her spot to tell others she's mine.
Must check out the woodchuck in his hole.
I can smell him down there. I'll get him yet.
I leave my word at his door and lift up my nose:
hmm—bitch on the wind. Can't resist that!
A whole new chapter, and he's shouting, "Come."
Better go to him, and then I'll escape.
I sit at his feet. I please—when it suits.
He's leashed me. The devil. I did what he said,
and the storyline was hotting up ever so well.
Oh, why am I tied to an illiterate man?

Called Down from the Sky

Razor thin wings
and needle-forked tail
descend the Caribbean blue,
until she circles at tree-height,
a Magnificent Frigate Bird,
visitor from the open sea.
She slips air, swoops down
to a sweet-water pond
and scoops bright water
in her great hooked beak.
Three times she lifts
over my head, three times
dips low and fills her bill
so close, I hear the thrupp
of torn water, see splintered drops
splash back in spangled agitation.
Thirst quenched, she climbs
the sky toward the coast—
pond still aquiver.

Autumn Encounter

I weed between the sugar water
and a Hummingbird's fierce desire.

A breath of feathers, the size of my pinky,
he sweeps in great pendulum arcs,

each time, hovering for a still second
before my face.

Wings thrumming, he pelts me
with curses,

scarlet throat flashing wicked
iridescence.

I withdraw, no match
for his massive irritation.

Conjuring Mary Oliver in Wolsfeld Woods

Poet, 1935 - 2019

The uncut woodland takes us in its arms,
and she's like a doe, white flag raised, until
she's within the comfort of maples and oaks.

Easier now, she drifts, silent as owl flight,
tread weightless on a trail of sodden leaves,
her passing like autumn mist in quiet air.

I follow, awkward—longing to converse,
but she's beyond company,
has no need for earnest admirers.

At a rotting stump of basswood, clad
with bracket fungus, she pauses and
tilts her nose to the scent of endings.

Further she slips into mossy woods,
where her form pales in the ochre light
of low sun, screened through fall maples.

It's time for me to let her be, as away
she planes between rough trunks, until
she's but a thought in uncut woodland.

Incubation

Through a sunrise window
I see a snapping turtle digging among
my petunias, baggy-trousered back legs
churning soft dirt, huge carapace

flattening flowers, her need, urgent.
The cavity, deep enough, she drops in
leathery eggs the size of ping-pong balls,
pedals her nest closed and leaves the sun

to do its work, nursing the darkness
summer-long in dirt's warm womb.
Then, one October day, a thought,
an inkling, an opening in the silence—

clawing upwards with penny-sized might,
something new and tender climbs into the light.

Bird and Conscience Converge

My friend, driving; me, beside her,
dreaming. "Stop!" I shout. "Stop."
She brakes, frightened. A refrigerator truck
howls past, horn blasting. I jump
from her car and run back fifty yards
to a still clump of fur, a bald eagle watching
from a white pine on the far side of the road.

Container trucks scissor past in both directions—
blades of speed between eagle and feast.
I grab the raccoon's back legs, wait
for an opening in the traffic and drag
the body across two lanes. A passing wag
yells, "Your dinner . . . ?" The eagle shifts,
perhaps disturbed by the same thought.

I roll the corpse down the road bank,
dodge trucks and cars back to my friend.
Emergency lights flashing, she stands,
hands on hips, shaking her head.
We watch the eagle spread dark wings,
swoop to feed below the road's far edge,
trailing shadows of hunger and evening.

Yesterday's Landscape

A triptych

The dog and I startle
a young buck sleeping
in a field of concealing grasses.
He bounds, haunches pumping
into yesterday's landscape—
his woodland clear-cut—
disturbed dirt, dug foundations,
skid steers and excavators.
I leash the dog, turn for home,
knowing his field will go next.

Driving to Red Lodge
across open prairie lands,
we stop twice—not for gas
but to scrape from the windshield
a paste of wasted lives—
grasshoppers, wasps, moths,
monarchs, mosquitoes,
beetles and bees,
essential lower orders.

Inviting as reality,
our generous picture-windows
reflect woodland in living image.
Below the windows,
a wing-splayed Oven Bird,
Goldfinch with bloodied beak,
Junco, head flopped sideways,
a clump of under-feathers
stuck to the pane.

Northern Lights

On a still night, we walk
to look for Aurora Borealis
as we did thirty years before,
when the countryside slept dark.

Now, new houses blaze,
lit for Christmas,
bleaching the Northern sky.
We shrug and turn for home—
stop dead—caught in an aurora
of wavering sound, howls
fierce and near. Neck hairs tingle—
we cling together, fearful
yet grateful for coyote cousins,
keepers of the early wild.

Trespass

Crystalline snow, grit hard, sings as it strikes the paper dry leaves of ironwood trees. Beyond the woods, a metallic river of sound sighs along County Road Six, and overhead, an airplane mumbles. No other sounds. I sit on a sawn oak stump in the hush of winter Big Woods. It's cold, but I'm unwilling to leave these great trees fastened in winter. Snow bastes rough trunks on their north-facing sides, and the leaves of ironwoods glow chestnut-red against so much whiteness. High in a linden, a red squirrel chatters like an old-fashioned sewing machine. Then quietens. Snow granules gather in my lap, toes ache, with brittle cold. I glance at my boots and note a humped line in the snow, where a deer mouse tunneled a road beneath concealing snow. Somewhere behind me, a pileated woodpecker bells an abrupt alarm, and a barred owl alights on a slender branch twenty feet away. It rides the dipping twig, pond-brown eyes locked on mine. Flustered, the owl flings upwards and lands beside the red squirrel, who breaks into staccato curses, scrambles down the linden trunk, loses footing and plummets into deep snow. The owl spreads ashy wings. Squirrel, still cursing, bolts into a hollow log. Crows erupt in a cacophony of aggression from the direction the owl has flown. Careless in rising, I trample the mouse tunnel and, as I retrace my snow-softened footsteps, crows subside, woods slip into silence.

Earth Casts Its Shadow Across the Moon

January 31, 2018, at 6:53 a.m.

Drowsy in dressing gown and boots, I idled along the driveway,
Cody's nose interpreting the happenings of the night.

Lifting my gaze from the dog's cheery tail, I chanced
to glance westward and saw through dark branches

a great orb, a bruised-looking eye, mottled
in shades of purple and ruby, its lens a brilliant disc of light

focused downwards, as though studying its parent, seeing
how Earth burns and suffocates in the smog of our needs,

the moon, itself, trespassed by our ambitions,
our planet home, burdened by our burgeoning demands.

I shivered. The moon's eye blinked shut.

When Our World Was Whole

At Sherburn National Wildlife Refuge

We near the refuge as skeins of moonlit mist lift
and we hear the music of a thousand cranes
roosting in the shallows of restored wetlands.
Behind us, the sun crests the horizon, feathering
white the needles of frost on reeds and grasses.

No wind, just the constant calling, as though
from distant beginnings in an Eocene dawn,
when creatures lived in common symmetry
before our coming. In a clamor of wild voices
cranes rise into morning on slow wings.

About the Author

Elizabeth Weir grew up in England and, in Miss Dyson's high school class, she read James Elroy Flecker's "Old Ships." The poet's use of imagery burned pictures on the screen of Weir's mind, and she stumbled upon Louis McNiece and Stephen Spender, both plumbing the unpredictability of the world. Coming to this country, she found Robert Frost, Mary Oliver and Ted Kooser, and an empty sheet of paper posed an invitation to her pencil that she could no longer resist.

Weir trained as a nurse and worked in London, Cape Town and in Minneapolis. In the Twin Cities, she wrote for local newspapers, reviewed theater in the Twin Cities for talkinbroadway.com and served on her city council, becoming the mayor. North Star Press of St. Cloud published her first book of poetry, *High on Table Mountain,* which was nominated for the 2017 Midwest Book Award.

Find Elizabeth online at www.elizabethvweir.com.